If it is allowed to live, a seal pup stays with
its mother until it can catch its own fish.
Seals are mammals and feed their babies with milk.
These are Weddell seals, which live in the Antarctic.

The most common seal is the harbour seal, which lives in the North Atlantic. It can sometimes be seen on the British coast. Seals spend a lot of time in the sea but come up on the beach to sunbathe.

Not all seals live where there are beaches.
These crabeater seals live in the Antarctic seas.
When they want to get out of the water
they haul themselves up on to an ice-floe.

The seal is perfectly designed for living in the water. It has a streamlined body with flippers and a short, strong tail. The true seal has no outer ears, unlike the fur seal and sea-lion.

Although seals are wonderful swimmers and divers, they have to come up for air sometimes. This Weddell seal can stay underwater for an hour. But then it must find a breathing-hole in the ice.

Flippers make swimming easier but are not so useful on the land as legs. Seals have to come out of the water to have their pups but it takes them a long time to move up the beach.

This elephant seal is using her flippers in a different way – to cover herself with sand. It is a way of keeping cool on a hot day, while the seal is out of the water.

It is easy to see how the elephant seal
got its name when you look at this male!
It is a southern elephant seal, snoozing.
It lives in the Antarctic with the penguins.

Like all members of the seal family, the male (called the bull) is much bigger than the female cow. Male elephant seals can weigh up to 2.5 tonnes, nearly four times as much as the female.

Sea-lions are members of the same family as seals. They are also mammals that feel at home in the water. These are California sea-lions, the kind you sometimes see in circuses.

These two Galapagos sea-lions are young males.
They are trying to find out which one is stronger.
You can see that the sea-lion's front flippers
are more like legs than the true seal's are.

Seals and sea-lions have to come on to dry land when they mate and have babies. The big dark sea-lion is the bull and he has lots of mates. They will all have his pups, usually only one each.

Once the sea-lion pup is born it feeds on its mother's milk, like a true seal. You can see that, unlike the true seal, the sea-lion pup has ears. This is the easiest way to tell the difference between a seal and a sea-lion.

Sea-lions that live in warm parts of the world, like these California ones, may get too hot even when they are in the water. So they use their flippers like fans to cool themselves down.

But sea-lions don't always mind being warm. Sometimes they like to lie in the sun. It helps to dry out the layer of thick under-fur that protects them against the cold when they are under water.

This under-fur is even thicker in the fur seals. They are closely related to sea-lions, as you can see by the ears, but are smaller. This pup will keep most of its fluffy fur when it grows up.

These young males look shaggy even when wet. Fur seals live in the northern and southern seas. These are from the Antarctic. All members of the seal family like playing in the water.

Walruses may not look like seals and sea-lions,
but they are part of the same family.
They also spend a lot of time in water but give
birth on beaches or, like these, on the ice.

Walruses are extremely sociable animals.
What you can see here are hundreds of walruses on the rocky beach of an island in Alaska.
You can probably just see their white tusks.

Both males and females have tusks and the males have very tough and knobbly skins. Can you see how pink they look? They are blushing to keep cool! The walrus is certainly the strangest member of the seal family.

Seals and sea-lions are very inquisitive. They are prepared to be friendly with people. But they eat a lot of fish, which makes them unpopular with people who catch fish for a living. Many are killed because of this as well as for their fur.

Index

eared seal	(see sea-lion and fur seal)
flipper	6, 8, 9, 13, 16
fur seal	18-19
sea-lion	title page, 12-17, 23
true seals – harp, Weddell, harbour, grey, elephant, crabeater –	front cover, 2-11
walrus	20-22, back cover

Measurements

kg = kilogram = 2.2 lbs

1 tonne = 1000 kg

Useful words about seals

breathing-hole	a hole in the ice, where seals can come up to breathe
bull	a male member of the seal family
cow	a female member of the seal family
lanugo	the fluffy fur of a new-born seal or sea-lion. It lasts about a month
mammal	a warm-blooded animal that gives birth to live young and feeds them with its own milk
pup	a baby seal, sea-lion or walrus
tusk	a kind of tooth that has become very long and tough, like the walrus's

First published 1987 by Belitha Press Limited, 31 Newington Green, London N16 9PU
in association with Methuen Children's Books Ltd, 11 New Fetter Lane, London EC4 4EE

Scientific Adviser: Dr Gwynne Vevers. Picture Researcher: Stella Martin. Design: Ken Hatherley
Acknowledgements are due to the following for the photographs used in this book: Bruce Coleman Ltd pp. 1, 2, 5, 14, 15, 16, 18, 20, 22, 23 and front cover; NHPA p. 12; Oxford Scientific Films Ltd pp. 3, 7 and 13; Frank Lane Picture Agency pp. 4, 8, 21 and back cover; Natural Science Photos p. 6; Survival Anglia pp. 9, 10, 11 and 19; Eric and David Hosking p. 17.

ISBN 0 416 01722 3 Printed in Hong Kong by South China Printing Co.

Dedicated to Sanjana, Shamamah and Shabiba